A Dive Into My Mind

Sarah Adedeji

BookLeaf Publishing

India | USA | UK

Presentation by *BookLeaf Publishing*

Web: www.bookleafpub.com

E-mail: info@bookleafpub.com

ISBN: 9789363315051

First edition 2023

DEDICATION

To everyone that has supported my writing.

ACKNOWLEDGEMENT

Thank you to the BookLeaf Publishing team who worked with me on this.

PREFACE

I find comfort in knowing that I am not alone in how I feel and that others, anywhere, share my emotions. I also find comfort in knowing that I write the words others struggle to put to their inner turmoil.

Introduction: The First Peek

Her tears collect around her
as she sinks down to her knees in surrender.
She clutches at her hair
as she struggles to understand the reason behind
her tears
and her body shakes with every violent sob;
as her breaths become ragged and hurried;
her thoughts whirl around in her brain;
and her thoughts torture her and
her caged demons rattle against her brain,
screaming at her and cackling menacingly -
warping her outlook on life.

Her hair fans out around her head
as she falls back onto the ground with laughter.
She clutches at her stomach
as she struggles to catch her breath whilst her
friends are in tears
and her body trembles with every silent chuckle;
her breaths become noisy and infrequent;
her thoughts lay dormant in her brain;
her thoughts refuse to play with her and
her caged demons retreat into the darkest abyss
of her mind,
agreeing not to punish her - allowing her to
relish in this moment that she's temporarily free.

The Popular Loner

You'll always find her in a crowd full of people;
a tactic devised to deceive the people
and a strategy applied to allude to the people
for, when she is without people,
there is none she can call her equal;
none she can call her people;
none with whom she can be feeble
and, to voice this, she is unable,
for many think it a fable,
believing many are at her table
to keep her fully stable
but those truly seated at her table
are the demons and the angels
that keep her unstable,
a party that remains invisible
while her smile is visible
and her eyes are miserable.

Happiness: A Concept

so foreign to me
but an emotion that I long to possess,
and my desire to experience it
I can no longer suppress.

Happiness: Nothing But

a fleeting moment for me,
and yet, I still crave its gentle touch
with a hunger that none can fathom
because of the diminishing soul
that it leaves behind;
always in a state worse than the last time
that it came to temporarily relieve me
of my own sick mind.

Night Terrors

And when the lights are turned down,
all the demons happily come out -
indeed, they are loud
cos they love to scream and shout
while, in the mind, they breed doubt
which is a task - paramount,
but when you flip that switch,
you'll soon come to realise that
the demons that feast on your highs
only live behind your eyes
underneath a beautiful disguise
and they love to play the mind
to leave you believing a lie
so, in the dark of the night,
to the demons, you comply,
and, in the light of the day,
with the demons, you play.

Heart, Stops

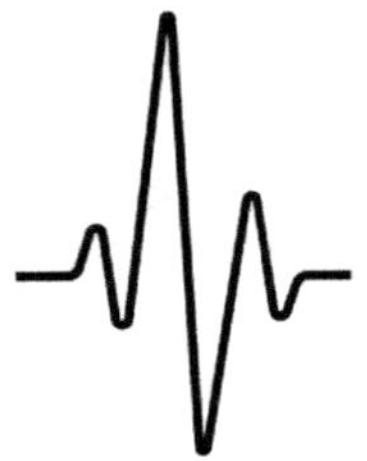

mouth, drops
eyes, pop
and all coherent thought
is completely
lost.

time, stops
pin, drops
fireworks, pop
and all the faith you've got
is completely
lost.

Movie

Everything feels like a movie
And yet, it's reality.

I'm the star of the show
And yet, I'm always pushed aside;
looking in from the outside
as if I'm watching through somebody else's
eyes;

Living a life that's not my own
and losing touch with myself.

Living a lie that's not my own
whilst strangled by a mental tie.

My mind wanders;
my body fatigues.

Time slows
And I am left
All alone.

Embedded

Your words have so deeply embedded
themselves into my mind that I can't help but to
act accordingly.

Because, slowly but surely,
I started to believe your cruel words,
And have now deemed myself as nothing but
worthless.

Slowly but surely,
I let your voice become my conscience,
And now I am hurting myself from within.

And, slowly but surely,
I lost sight of my true worth,
And now I am nothing but the shell of who I was
And the physical representation of your sick and
twisted words.

Entity

Somewhere inside of me,
there is this entity,
that has complete control over my entirety,
and as it rots inside of me,
it keeps me away from sobriety.

I try to destroy it,
but as it grows internally,
I resort to hurting myself externally
and now I've come to realise
that it's my fate to suffer eternally.

How Did I Get Here?

No, tell me!

How did I get into another episode of despair yet
again?
Filled with a loneliness that many could not bear
and a brokenness that I cannot repair
but can still deftly conceal from everyone's glare
with style and flair, for none seem to care
whenever I try to share but now I wouldn't even
dare;
instead finding solitude in my personal lair
that was, at first,
a place of which I warned myself to beware,
but now is a beautiful nightmare in which I shed
a tear
every time I am there for no one else is here
to free me from this wretched nightmare
that has now become a regular affair.

Periscope

Whilst submerged in her darkest self,
she peeps through her periscope
and silently observes the happiness
that's just right out of her reach.

And,
as she floats in the never-ending nothingness;
surrounded by entities that only exist in the dark,
she mulls over the countless escape strategies
that have failed her time and time again,
wondering where she's going wrong,
and begins to believe that maybe,
just maybe,
she doesn't deserve that happiness.

At Its Finest

It's like a bat's cave where the words echo,
slowly chipping at the wall that represents my
stability and sanity.

It's like a straitjacket where the words are
trapped,
allowed no escape.

It's like a prison cell where the words are
isolated,
slowly chipping at the hope that represents my
freedom.

Wait, can you hear that?
Yeah, no, me neither.
Because that's silent suffering at its finest.
Silent pain at its finest.
Silent isolation at its finest.

I can no longer put a timestamp on the
disappearance,
or, rather, the taming of these thoughts.

Wait, can you see that?
Yeah, no, me neither.
Because that's dwindling strength at its finest.
That's dwindling oxygen at its finest.
That's dwindling light at its finest.

I can no longer see through the confusion - the
blur.

Different Persona

Each day is a different persona
just to keep people satisfied
and each day is a different you
just to stay in their good books.

They see you smile but they don't know what's
going on inside
and they see you smile but they don't know that,
while you're going left, right, front, back,
you're dying inside.

They see you smile but they don't know that
you're always placing a new you on top of the
old ones that have expired.
But when will you ever place the real you on
top?

Because it's rotting underneath all your facades
and screaming for an escape.

Fighting to Survive

Before even beginning to heal,
they're already helping others to heal,
a process in which they lose all ability to feel
led by the common misconception
that their struggle is defined by external
perception
which then leaves them to fight an internal war
whilst finding themselves on the frontline of a
conflict not their own
but what greater purpose does this serve?
they gain battle scars ingrained further than the
skin that are never to be seen
beyond the surface and isn't it ironic how we
have sight
but still cannot see the deeper things in life
where man and demon are very much alike
as to how they can infiltrate your mind
but none of them you can fight
without it costing you your life
but there's comfort in the fact
that many before have tried
with a bit more luck each time
so, one can only hope
that they are now wise,
wise enough to survive.

Day in

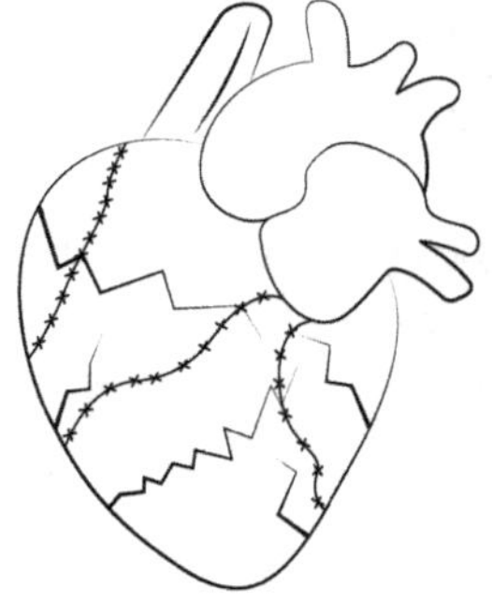

and day out,
they work tirelessly
to put everyone's hearts
back into one piece
while, somewhere no one can see,
their own remains shattered in piece -s,
so, to maintain appearances,
in the hole, where her heart should sit, sits
the mould of perseverance
and gathered bobs and bits,
which, thankfully, bear resemblance
to the heart that used to beat.

Numb

Is it overwhelmingly numb?
Or is it numbingly overwhelming?

Either way, it doesn't matter because
still, they couldn't word
just exactly how they were feeling
and all that they could tell you was,
somehow,
they had managed to
enter this state of indifference
where they still felt everything and
believed in their own insignificance;
where intense waves of emotions visited them,
regularly immobilising them
as they tried to detach themselves
from the searing pain that had consumed them
and gave them an inexplainable feeling
of numbness and sensitivity
that exceeded their emotional capacity
and took over their mental activity.

Hers vs Theirs

Heaviness is all that she can feel

as her temples pulse with pain

and as her eyes fade with fear

and as her arms droop with dread.

Insistent headaches are drowned

by consistent music and

blank stares in the mirror are followed

by bright smiles in the camera.

Her burdens keep her in bed

but their burdens keep her out of it

and her burdens physically restrain her

but their burdens, they –

they free her in some ironic and twisted way.

Heaviness is all that she can feel

as her mind throbs with thoughts

and as her cheeks pale with pensiveness

and as her shoulders fall with fogginess.

But,

in a blink of an eye,

her shoulders are pushed back with purpose

and her eyes are bright with bliss

and her arms are animated with ambition.

Fake It Til You Make It

She walks with her head up high,

and pride in her stride,

and her face, it shines

with the brightest of smiles

to cleverly hide what's truly inside

as she walks with her heart extremely low,

with pain spreading through her torso,

and her eyes guard her tormented soul

while she questions why her mind is so cold

and she walks with a pep in her step,

and her stomach full of dread,

and with voices in her head,

waiting for it all to come to an end.

The Silent Chronic Death

As time goes past,

she continually adjusts her mask

so that whoever she may pass

will never see the bad,

but only the good,

and, while she cracks

underneath the burden on her back,

she stays on the right track;

always walking upright

so that the wool around people's eyes

will always stay wrapped

so that they continue to be blind

to her slow defeat to her internal fight.

Inbuilt Dam

Her inbuilt dam shudders

at the sudden inflow of tears

and her heartbeat flutters

at the pain inflicted by others.

Her upper lip quivers,

and her entire face reddens

but, still, her inbuilt dam decides to remain
stubborn

until something so foreign

takes residence on its southern.

And then, slowly but surely,

the unwanted crack

multiplies and expands

to open up gaps

that act as leaky taps

and, just like that,

her inbuilt dam snaps.

All those tears then push past the broken dam

and rush out of her eyes to race each other by

jumping off her lashes and sliding down her
cheeks,

and nothing visual is left behind,

not even salty streaks,

but somewhere behind her eyes,

is a broken dam that creaks,

reaching for all its pieces,

as she momentarily allows herself to be weak.

And then just like that,

she's back in one piece.

Will I Ever Be Free?

Whilst feeling locked in and lost in the rough
scene

of your daily routine, you watch your life
dangerously careen

from places you're not meant to be in

to places you're meant to experience

but, as you sit in between

the person you've already been

and the person you're supposed to be,

you slowly lose the ability to see that you too
will someday be free.

Design

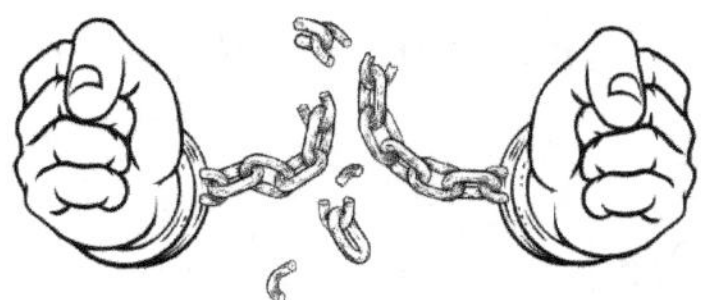

Trying to overcome my mind to rewrite its
design

whilst, in it, I am confined, is a task unkind.

Trying to overcome my mind to have it rewired

before it's expired, is a task of which completion
is desired.

Trying to overcome my mind means, from it, I
have to unbind

and, to it, I have to define happiness, divine,

so, itself it can refine and, with the hopes that
it'll realign,

to the joy waiting in line, I leave all my chains
behind

to escape from this mind of mine.